# 10 Quantum Jumps In Innovation

Paramendra Kumar Bhagat

Identifying the top 10 quantum jumps in business and technology throughout history is subjective and depends on the perspective of the evaluator. Here's a broad consensus of milestones that fundamentally transformed human society and economy:

**Introduction: The Quantum Leaps Of Innovation (Page 6)**

**1. The Agricultural Revolution (~10,000 BCE) (Page 8)**

- **Innovation**: The domestication of plants and animals.
- **Impact**: Transition from hunter-gatherer societies to settled agricultural communities, enabling population growth, urbanization, and the foundation of trade and commerce.

**2. The Invention of Writing (~3200 BCE) (Page 15)**

- **Innovation**: Development of written scripts like cuneiform and hieroglyphics.
- **Impact**: Enabled record-keeping, complex administration, and the birth of formalized trade and financial systems.

**3. The Industrial Revolution (18th-19th Century) (Page 21)**

- **Innovation**: Mechanization of production using steam power and machinery.

- **Impact**: Massive increases in productivity, urbanization, and the development of modern capitalism and global trade networks.

### 4. The Development of Electricity (19th Century) (Page 29)

- **Innovation**: Harnessing electricity for industrial and domestic use.
- **Impact**: Revolutionized industry, communication, and everyday life with innovations like the light bulb, electric motors, and telecommunications.

### 5. The Invention of the Telephone (1876) (Page 36)

- **Innovation**: Alexander Graham Bell's invention of the telephone.
- **Impact**: Revolutionized communication, enabling instant connectivity over long distances, laying the groundwork for modern communication networks.

### 6. The Digital Revolution (20th Century) (Page 44)

- **Innovation**: The advent of computers, semiconductors, and digital technology.
- **Impact**: Transformed every industry through data processing, automation, and the creation of the internet.

### 7. The Internet Revolution (1990s) (Page 52)

- **Innovation**: The development of the World Wide Web and global connectivity.
- **Impact**: Democratized access to information, enabled e-commerce, social media, and new business models like the gig economy.

### 8. The Green Revolution (Mid-20th Century) (Page 60)

- **Innovation**: Advances in agricultural science, such as high-yield crops and synthetic fertilizers.
- **Impact**: Alleviated food shortages in many parts of the world, enabling population growth and stability.

## 9. Artificial Intelligence and Machine Learning (21st Century) (Page 68)

- **Innovation**: Development of algorithms and computational power to enable AI.
- **Impact**: Transformed industries from healthcare to finance, enabling automation, predictive analytics, and personalized services.

## 10. Quantum Computing (Emerging) (Page 76)

- **Innovation**: Harnessing quantum mechanics for computing.
- **Impact**: Potential to solve complex problems in cryptography, material science, and pharmaceuticals at an unprecedented scale.

Each of these jumps introduced new paradigms, enabling societies to operate more efficiently and unlocking previously inconceivable possibilities.

## Introduction: The Quantum Leaps of Innovation

Throughout human history, certain innovations have redefined the trajectory of civilization, propelling societies into new paradigms of thought, productivity, and interaction. This book explores ten transformative milestones in the history of business and technology, each representing a quantum leap that revolutionized the way we live, work, and connect. From the Agricultural Revolution, where the domestication of plants and animals laid the foundation for settled societies, to the invention of writing, which enabled record-keeping and complex administration, these early advancements marked the beginnings of human progress. The Industrial Revolution brought mechanization and steam power, heralding unprecedented productivity and urbanization. Meanwhile, the harnessing of electricity in the 19th century illuminated homes, powered industries, and catalyzed modern communication.

The 20th and 21st centuries have witnessed a series of rapid, interconnected innovations that continue to shape the modern world. The telephone revolutionized instant connectivity, while the Digital Revolution introduced computers, semiconductors, and the internet, fundamentally altering every industry. The Green Revolution addressed global food security through agricultural science, and Artificial Intelligence and Machine Learning are now transforming healthcare, finance, and personalized services. Most recently, the Internet Revolution democratized information and commerce, and the emerging field of Quantum Computing holds promise to solve complex problems in cryptography, material science, and beyond. Each chapter delves into these groundbreaking innovations, analyzing their origins, societal impacts, and the lessons they offer for navigating future challenges. Together, these stories illustrate humanity's relentless pursuit of progress and the boundless potential of human ingenuity.

## The Agricultural Revolution: A Turning Point in Human History

The Agricultural Revolution, often referred to as the Neolithic Revolution, marks one of the most transformative periods in human history. Occurring around 10,000 BCE, this era saw humans transition from nomadic hunter-gatherer societies to settled agricultural communities. This fundamental shift laid the groundwork for the development of civilization as we know it today. The revolution not only transformed the way humans interacted with their environment but also instigated profound changes in social structures, economic systems, and cultural practices. In this essay, we will explore the causes, innovations, consequences, and enduring legacy of the Agricultural Revolution in detail.

## 1. The Pre-Agricultural World

Before the Agricultural Revolution, human societies were primarily hunter-gatherers. These groups relied on hunting animals, fishing, and gathering wild plants for sustenance. Their survival depended heavily on environmental factors, such as the availability of natural resources and climatic conditions. Nomadic lifestyles were a necessity, as people moved to follow migrating herds and seasonal growth of plants.

The population density of these groups was relatively low, as the carrying capacity of the land limited the number of individuals it could support. Social structures were typically egalitarian, with roles defined by necessity rather than hierarchy. Cultural practices, including art, music, and rituals, were deeply tied to the natural world and the cycles of life and death.

Despite its apparent simplicity, this way of life was highly adaptive and sustainable for thousands of years. However, a confluence of factors, including climate change and increasing population pressures, began to challenge this model, necessitating innovation.

## 2. Causes of the Agricultural Revolution

Several interconnected factors contributed to the emergence of agriculture. One primary driver was the climatic changes at the end of the last Ice Age, around 12,000 years ago. This period, known as the Holocene Epoch, brought about a more stable and warmer climate, which made certain regions, such as the Fertile Crescent in the Middle East, particularly conducive to plant and animal domestication.

Another factor was the increasing population density in some areas, which put pressure on existing resources. As hunting large game became less reliable and gathering wild plants could no longer meet the needs of growing communities, humans began experimenting with cultivating plants and domesticating animals.

Cultural and technological advancements also played a role. The development of tools, such as sickles and grinding stones, made it easier to harvest and process plant materials. Additionally, humans' growing knowledge of the life cycles of plants and animals enabled them to manipulate these processes for their benefit.

## 3. Key Innovations of the Agricultural Revolution

The Agricultural Revolution was characterized by several groundbreaking innovations that fundamentally altered human societies:

### Domestication of Plants and Animals

The domestication of plants involved selecting and cultivating crops that were more productive, nutritious, and easier to harvest. Early domesticated crops included wheat, barley, rice, maize, and legumes. Similarly, the domestication of animals provided reliable sources of meat, milk, hides, and labor. Key domesticated animals included sheep, goats, cattle, and pigs.

### Irrigation and Water Management

To support agriculture, early farmers developed irrigation techniques to control water supply. This was especially critical in regions with variable rainfall. Systems of canals, ditches, and reservoirs allowed for the cultivation of crops in otherwise arid areas, significantly expanding the range of habitable and farmable land.

### Tool Development

Agriculture necessitated new tools and technologies. Early farmers used plows to till the soil, hoes to weed, and grinding stones to process grains. Over time, these tools became more sophisticated, facilitating greater efficiency and productivity.

**Permanent Settlements**

The shift to agriculture encouraged the establishment of permanent settlements. Villages like Jericho and Çatalhöyük are among the earliest known examples of such communities, featuring dwellings, storage facilities, and communal spaces.

## 4. Social and Economic Consequences

The Agricultural Revolution triggered a cascade of changes in human societies, reshaping social hierarchies, economic systems, and cultural practices:

**Population Growth**

Agriculture supported larger populations by providing a more stable and predictable food supply. As food surpluses became possible, communities grew in size, eventually leading to the development of towns and cities.

**Social Stratification**

The surplus generated by agriculture also led to the emergence of social hierarchies. Not everyone needed to be involved in food production, allowing some individuals to specialize in other roles, such as artisans, traders, and leaders. This division of labor paved the way for complex societies but also created disparities in wealth and power.

**Trade and Economic Networks**

Surplus food and specialized goods encouraged the development of trade networks. Early trade involved the exchange of agricultural products, tools, and luxury items like obsidian, shells, and ornaments. These exchanges connected distant communities and facilitated cultural diffusion.

**Property and Land Ownership**

Agriculture introduced the concept of land ownership, as individuals and families claimed plots for cultivation. This shift had profound implications for social organization and conflict, as disputes over land and resources became common.

## 5. Cultural and Ideological Shifts

The Agricultural Revolution also influenced cultural and ideological practices. The relationship between humans and the environment became more controlled and exploitative, reflected in religious and mythological narratives that emphasized human dominion over nature. Temples and other monumental structures, such as those found at Göbekli Tepe, suggest a close connection between agriculture, religion, and social organization.

Writing systems and record-keeping emerged in part to manage agricultural surpluses and trade. Early scripts, such as cuneiform, were used to document transactions, land ownership, and harvests, laying the foundation for modern bureaucracies.

## 6. Environmental Impact

While the Agricultural Revolution brought numerous benefits, it also had significant environmental consequences. Deforestation, soil degradation, and the loss of biodiversity were direct results of agricultural expansion. Irrigation systems, while innovative, often led to salinization and long-term fertility issues. These challenges underscore the complex relationship between human progress and environmental sustainability.

## 7. The Agricultural Revolution's Legacy

The impact of the Agricultural Revolution is still evident today. Modern agriculture, with its reliance on domesticated crops and animals, is a direct descendant of the innovations of this era. The principles of irrigation, land management, and food storage established during this time continue to underpin contemporary agricultural practices.

Moreover, the revolution set humanity on a trajectory toward urbanization, industrialization, and globalization. The development of surplus food allowed for the growth of civilizations, the rise of empires, and the eventual emergence of modern nation-states.

## 8. Criticisms and Reassessments

Recent scholarship has questioned the unqualified benefits of the Agricultural Revolution. Some argue that the shift to agriculture resulted in greater inequality, increased labor demands, and a decline in overall health compared to hunter-gatherer societies. Skeletal evidence suggests that early agriculturalists experienced higher rates of malnutrition and disease due to reliance on a narrower range of foods and the close proximity of humans and animals.

However, despite these critiques, the Agricultural Revolution remains a pivotal moment in human history, marking the beginning of a journey that has led to unprecedented levels of technological and cultural achievement.

## 9. Conclusion

The Agricultural Revolution was a quantum leap in human development. It transformed the way humans lived, worked, and interacted with their environment, laying the foundation for the complex societies we inhabit today. While it brought challenges and new forms of inequality, its innovations enabled the growth of civilizations and the vast array of cultural and technological advancements that followed. By understanding this transformative period, we gain valuable insights into the origins of our modern world and the enduring interplay between humanity and the natural world.

# The Invention of Writing: Humanity's Quantum Leap

## Introduction: Writing as the Catalyst of Civilization

The invention of writing, occurring around 3200 BCE, represents one of the most significant milestones in human history. It is not merely a technological innovation but a profound transformation in the way humanity communicates, organizes, and understands the world. Writing systems like cuneiform in Mesopotamia and hieroglyphics in Egypt did more than record information; they became the bedrock of administration, trade, culture, and the historical record. This essay explores the origins, development, and enduring impact of writing, emphasizing its role as a catalyst for civilization.

## 1. The Pre-Writing Era: Oral Traditions and Their Limitations

Before the advent of writing, human communication and cultural transmission relied on oral traditions. Stories, laws, and knowledge were passed down verbally from generation to generation. While oral traditions were effective in preserving culture and fostering communal bonds, they had significant limitations.

**Memory and Accuracy**

Oral traditions were susceptible to the fragility of human memory. Over time, stories and laws could be distorted or lost, especially in the absence of systematic mechanisms for recall.

**Scope and Scale**

Complex societies require more than oral memory to function effectively. As communities grew larger and more interconnected, the need for precise record-keeping, long-term storage of information, and communication across distances became critical.

**Economic and Administrative Challenges**

Trade, taxation, and governance demanded accurate and standardized records. Without writing, managing resources, enforcing contracts, and planning infrastructure were cumbersome and prone to error.

## 2. The Birth of Writing: Cuneiform and Hieroglyphics

The first writing systems emerged independently in different parts of the world, most notably in Mesopotamia and Egypt. While the exact timeline varies, both systems began as practical tools for record-keeping and evolved into sophisticated means of communication.

## Cuneiform: The First Writing System

Cuneiform, developed by the Sumerians around 3200 BCE, is widely regarded as the world's first writing system. It began as pictograms inscribed on clay tablets and gradually became more abstract and symbolic.

- **Purpose**: Initially used for accounting, cuneiform recorded transactions, inventories, and taxes. Over time, it expanded to encompass legal codes, literature, and administrative decrees.
- **Medium**: Clay tablets were durable and widely available, making them ideal for preserving written records.
- **Evolution**: As the script evolved, it became more efficient and versatile, enabling the recording of complex ideas and narratives.

## Hieroglyphics: The Sacred Writing of Egypt

Around the same time as cuneiform, the Egyptians developed hieroglyphics, a writing system that combined pictorial and phonetic elements.

- **Purpose**: Hieroglyphics served both practical and ceremonial purposes, appearing on monuments, tombs, and administrative documents.
- **Medium**: Papyrus, a paper-like material made from the papyrus plant, complemented stone carvings as a medium for writing.
- **Symbolism**: Unlike cuneiform, hieroglyphics retained strong visual and symbolic qualities, reflecting Egypt's religious and cultural ethos.

# 3. The Functions of Writing: Record-Keeping and Beyond

The initial purpose of writing was utilitarian, addressing the needs of growing urban societies. However, its functions quickly expanded, influencing every facet of civilization.

**Record-Keeping**

Writing solved the problem of maintaining accurate and permanent records. In Mesopotamia, temple administrators used cuneiform to track grain supplies, livestock, and labor allocations. Similarly, Egyptian scribes documented harvests, taxes, and military campaigns.

**Complex Administration**

Writing enabled the development of bureaucracies. Laws, decrees, and contracts could be codified, ensuring consistency and fairness in governance. The Code of Hammurabi, inscribed in cuneiform, stands as a testament to the power of written law.

**Trade and Financial Systems**

The expansion of trade networks necessitated reliable systems for recording transactions. Writing facilitated the creation of contracts, inventories, and receipts, laying the groundwork for modern economic systems. Merchants in Mesopotamia, for instance, used cuneiform to document trade agreements and manage accounts.

**Cultural Preservation and Transmission**

Writing became a repository for cultural knowledge. Myths, religious texts, and historical records were written down, preserving them for future generations. Works like the *Epic of Gilgamesh* in Mesopotamia and the *Book of the Dead* in Egypt highlight the cultural richness made possible by writing.

## 4. The Impact on Society: A Catalyst for Complexity

The invention of writing transformed societies in profound ways, enabling the rise of complex civilizations.

## Urbanization and State Formation

Writing facilitated the administration of large populations and territories. It enabled the collection of taxes, organization of labor, and planning of infrastructure projects, driving urbanization and the formation of states.

## Social Stratification

The ability to read and write became a marker of status. Scribes and scholars held privileged positions, while access to education became a tool for social mobility or control.

## Knowledge Expansion

Writing accelerated the accumulation and dissemination of knowledge. Early scientific, mathematical, and medical texts laid the foundation for future advancements, transforming how societies understood and interacted with the world.

# 5. Writing and the Evolution of Language

The development of writing influenced the evolution of spoken language. Written systems preserved linguistic structures and vocabulary, providing a stable framework for communication across generations. They also introduced standardization, as seen in the creation of official scripts and dialects.

## Phonetic Scripts and Alphabets

Over time, writing systems became more accessible. The development of alphabets, such as the Phoenician script, simplified writing, enabling broader literacy and facilitating the spread of ideas.

### Linguistic Diversity

While early writing systems were limited to elite classes, they preserved linguistic diversity. Texts in various languages provide invaluable insights into ancient cultures and their interactions.

## 6. The Legacy of Writing

The invention of writing remains one of humanity's most enduring achievements. Its impact is evident in the foundations of modern society.

### The Historical Record

Writing allows us to study and understand the past. Ancient texts provide insights into early civilizations, their beliefs, and their achievements, bridging the gap between history and archaeology.

### Cultural Continuity

Through written records, cultures preserve their identities, values, and traditions. From religious scriptures to literary classics, writing ensures that cultural legacies endure.

### Innovation and Progress

The written word drives innovation. From the invention of the printing press to the digital revolution, writing has continually evolved, shaping how we share and consume information.

## 7. Critiques and Challenges

While writing has transformed human society, it has also introduced challenges. Early writing systems reinforced social hierarchies, with literacy often confined to elite classes. Additionally, the reliance on written records can marginalize oral traditions and non-literate cultures.

**Preservation and Accessibility**

The fragility of early writing materials, such as clay tablets and papyrus, poses challenges for preservation. Efforts to digitize ancient texts highlight the ongoing struggle to make historical records accessible to all.

**Ethical Considerations**

The power of writing to shape narratives raises ethical questions. Historical records often reflect the perspectives of dominant groups, necessitating critical examination to uncover marginalized voices.

## Conclusion: Writing as Humanity's Quantum Leap

The invention of writing represents a quantum leap in human development, transforming how societies organize, communicate, and evolve. From its humble beginnings as a tool for record-keeping, writing has become a cornerstone of civilization, enabling cultural preservation, knowledge expansion, and social progress. As we continue to innovate and adapt writing to new technologies, its legacy reminds us of our shared humanity and the enduring power of the written word.

## The Industrial Revolution: Transforming Society and Shaping the Modern World

## Introduction: The Dawn of a New Era

The Industrial Revolution, spanning the 18th and 19th centuries, stands as one of the most transformative periods in human history. Characterized by the mechanization of production, the widespread use of steam power, and the rise of machinery, it marked a radical departure from agrarian economies and traditional methods of production. This era not only revolutionized industries but also reshaped societies, economies, and the global order. This essay explores the innovations, drivers, and far-reaching impacts of the Industrial Revolution, delving into its legacy and lessons for the modern world.

# 1. The Pre-Industrial World: Foundations of Change

### Agrarian Economies

Before the Industrial Revolution, most economies were predominantly agrarian. The vast majority of people lived in rural areas, working as farmers, artisans, or small-scale traders. Production was labor-intensive, and goods were crafted by hand or using simple tools.

### Cottage Industries and Limitations

Small-scale industries, often operating out of homes or small workshops, played a role in supplementing agricultural income. These "cottage industries" were limited by the inefficiency of manual labor and the lack of technological advancements, making mass production impractical.

### Economic and Population Growth

The 17th and early 18th centuries witnessed gradual economic growth and a rising population, creating increased demand for goods. However, traditional production methods struggled to meet this demand, setting the stage for transformative change.

# 2. Key Innovations of the Industrial Revolution

The Industrial Revolution was driven by groundbreaking innovations that redefined production processes and economic systems.

### Steam Power

The invention of the steam engine by innovators like Thomas Newcomen and James Watt revolutionized energy use. Steam engines became the driving force behind industrial machinery, transportation, and manufacturing processes.

### Mechanization and Machinery

The introduction of machinery, such as the spinning jenny, power loom, and cotton gin, revolutionized textile production. These machines drastically increased productivity and reduced the reliance on manual labor.

### Iron and Steel Production

Advancements in metallurgy, such as the Bessemer process, allowed for the mass production of iron and steel. These materials were essential for building machinery, railways, and infrastructure.

### Transportation Innovations

The development of canals, railways, and steam-powered ships facilitated the efficient movement of goods and people, connecting markets and driving economic expansion.

### Communication Advances

Inventions like the telegraph revolutionized communication, enabling instant information exchange across vast distances and fostering global connectivity.

## 3. The Drivers of Industrialization

Several factors contributed to the emergence and spread of the Industrial Revolution.

### Natural Resources

Abundant coal and iron reserves in countries like Britain provided the raw materials and energy needed for industrialization.

### Economic Policies

The growth of capitalism, supported by policies promoting trade and innovation, created an environment conducive to industrial growth. Governments and private investors financed infrastructure projects and industrial ventures.

**Scientific and Technological Advancements**

The Enlightenment's emphasis on science and innovation fostered a culture of experimentation and discovery, leading to technological breakthroughs.

**Labor Supply**

The population growth of the 18th century provided a surplus labor force, essential for manning factories and supporting industrial expansion.

## 4. Social and Economic Impacts

The Industrial Revolution brought about profound changes in society and the economy, transforming nearly every aspect of life.

**Urbanization**

The rise of factories led to mass migration from rural areas to cities. Urban centers grew rapidly, often outpacing the development of infrastructure and services, resulting in overcrowding and challenging living conditions.

**Economic Growth and Productivity**

Mechanized production dramatically increased efficiency and output. This growth fueled wealth creation, expanded markets, and laid the foundations for modern capitalism.

**Changes in Labor**

The shift from agrarian work to industrial labor marked a significant transformation in employment. Factory work introduced regimented schedules and repetitive tasks, fundamentally altering workers' relationships with time and labor.

**Social Stratification**

While industrialization created immense wealth, it also deepened social inequalities. Factory owners and industrialists amassed fortunes, while many workers endured low wages, long hours, and hazardous conditions.

**Global Trade Networks**

The Industrial Revolution expanded global trade, integrating economies and fostering interdependence. Manufactured goods from industrialized nations were exported worldwide, often displacing traditional industries in less industrialized regions.

## 5. Cultural and Intellectual Shifts

The Industrial Revolution influenced not only material conditions but also cultural and intellectual landscapes.

**Rise of Consumer Culture**

The increased availability of goods and the growth of disposable income contributed to the emergence of a consumer-oriented society. Mass production made goods more affordable, creating new markets and consumption patterns.

**Education and Skill Development**

Industrialization underscored the importance of education and specialized skills. Technical schools and institutions emerged to train workers and engineers, fostering innovation and progress.

**Artistic and Literary Responses**

The Industrial Revolution inspired diverse artistic and literary responses. Romanticism, for example, celebrated nature and critiqued industrialization's impact on the environment and human spirit. Writers like Charles Dickens highlighted the social issues and inequalities of industrial society.

## 6. Challenges and Critiques

While the Industrial Revolution brought unprecedented progress, it also posed significant challenges and sparked critiques.

### Environmental Degradation

Industrial activities led to deforestation, pollution, and the exploitation of natural resources. The environmental consequences of industrialization remain a pressing concern today.

### Worker Exploitation

Factory workers faced harsh conditions, including long hours, low wages, and unsafe environments. The rise of labor unions and movements for workers' rights was a direct response to these challenges.

### Global Inequalities

Industrialization created disparities between industrialized and non-industrialized regions. Colonization and resource extraction often exacerbated these inequalities, shaping global power dynamics.

## 7. The Legacy of the Industrial Revolution

The Industrial Revolution's legacy is multifaceted, influencing every aspect of modern life.

### Technological Progress

The innovations of the Industrial Revolution laid the groundwork for subsequent technological advancements, from the electric age to the digital revolution.

### Economic Transformation

Industrialization established the framework for modern economies, characterized by mass production, global trade, and capitalist systems.

### Urbanization and Demographic Shifts

The growth of cities and changes in population dynamics continue to shape contemporary societies, influencing urban planning, housing, and infrastructure.

### Social Reforms

The challenges of industrialization spurred social reforms and movements, including labor laws, public health initiatives, and environmental conservation efforts.

## 8. Lessons for the Future

The Industrial Revolution offers valuable lessons for navigating the challenges of modern technological and societal transformations.

### Balancing Progress and Sustainability

The environmental consequences of industrialization highlight the need for sustainable development practices that balance progress with ecological stewardship.

### Addressing Inequalities

Ensuring equitable distribution of the benefits of innovation requires proactive policies and inclusive approaches.

**Fostering Innovation and Adaptation**

The spirit of innovation that drove the Industrial Revolution remains essential for addressing contemporary challenges, from climate change to global health crises.

## Conclusion: A Revolution That Shaped the World

The Industrial Revolution was more than a period of technological change; it was a transformative era that reshaped societies, economies, and cultures. Its innovations and impacts continue to influence the modern world, offering both opportunities and challenges. By reflecting on the lessons of this pivotal era, humanity can strive to harness the power of progress while addressing the complexities of an interconnected and rapidly evolving world.

## The Development of Electricity: Illuminating the Path to Modernity

### Introduction: The Spark That Transformed the World

The 19th century witnessed a transformative leap with the development of electricity. This innovation, encompassing the generation, distribution, and application of electrical energy, revolutionized industry, communication, and daily life. From the invention of the light bulb to the advent of telecommunications, electricity became the cornerstone of modern civilization. This essay explores the historical context, key innovations, societal impacts, and enduring legacy of electricity, tracing its journey from experimental curiosity to a ubiquitous force shaping the contemporary world.

## 1. The Pre-Electric Era: A World Without Wires

Before the advent of electricity, human societies relied on traditional sources of energy such as fire, water, wind, and manual labor. These energy systems, while effective for millennia, had limitations that constrained technological and economic development.

**Energy Sources and Limitations**

- **Candlelight and Oil Lamps**: Illumination depended on fire-based sources, which were inefficient and hazardous.
- **Water and Wind Power**: While powering mills and machinery, these sources were geographically constrained and weather-dependent.
- **Manual and Animal Labor**: Labor-intensive processes limited productivity and economic scalability.

**Early Experiments with Electricity**

The pre-19th century saw notable advancements in understanding electricity as a natural phenomenon. Pioneers like Benjamin Franklin, Alessandro Volta, and Michael Faraday laid the groundwork for practical applications by studying electrical charge, batteries, and electromagnetic induction.

## 2. Breakthrough Innovations in Electricity

The 19th century was marked by groundbreaking inventions that harnessed electricity for practical use, transforming theoretical science into tangible technology.

**The Light Bulb: Illuminating Homes and Workplaces**

Thomas Edison's invention of the practical incandescent light bulb in 1879 symbolized the transition to electrically powered illumination. While others like Joseph Swan contributed to its development, Edison's integration of the bulb with an electrical distribution system made widespread adoption feasible.

- **Impact on Society**: Extended working hours, enhanced safety, and reduced reliance on fire-based lighting.
- **Industrial Applications**: Factories operated efficiently with artificial lighting, increasing productivity.

**Electric Motors: Powering Machines and Transportation**

The development of electric motors, pioneered by Nikola Tesla and others, enabled electricity to drive machinery and vehicles.

- **Industrial Impact**: Replaced steam engines, allowing for cleaner and more efficient factories.
- **Transportation**: Powered electric trains, trolleys, and, later, cars, revolutionizing mobility.

**Telecommunications: Connecting the World**

The application of electricity to communication transformed global connectivity. Samuel Morse's telegraph (1837) and Alexander Graham Bell's telephone (1876) utilized electrical signals to transmit messages instantly.

- **Economic Implications**: Facilitated rapid business transactions and information exchange.
- **Cultural Impact**: Shrunk perceived distances, fostering a sense of global community.

## 3. Building the Infrastructure: Electrification of Society

The widespread adoption of electricity required the development of robust infrastructure for generation, transmission, and distribution.

**Power Generation**

- **Hydroelectric Power**: Early hydroelectric plants harnessed water to generate electricity, exemplified by the Niagara Falls power station (1895).
- **Thermal Power**: Coal-fired power plants became a dominant source of electricity, driving industrial growth.

**Electrical Grids**

- **AC vs. DC Systems**: The rivalry between Tesla's alternating current (AC) and Edison's direct current (DC) shaped the modern electrical grid. AC's efficiency over long distances ensured its dominance.
- **Urban Electrification**: Cities became hubs of electrification, with electric streetlights and tram systems transforming urban landscapes.

**Appliances and Consumer Goods**

Electricity spurred the creation of household appliances, such as electric stoves, refrigerators, and washing machines, improving daily life and fostering consumer culture.

## 4. Social and Economic Impacts

The development of electricity catalyzed profound changes in social structures, economic systems, and cultural practices.

**Industrial Productivity**

- **Automation**: Electrically powered machines automated production, reducing costs and increasing output.
- **Factory Efficiency**: Electrification enabled centralized power sources, optimizing industrial workflows.

**Urbanization**

- **Modern Cities**: Electrification spurred the growth of urban centers, with electric lighting, transportation, and infrastructure defining modern cities.
- **Migration**: People moved to electrified areas in search of opportunities, accelerating urbanization.

### Quality of Life

- **Health and Safety**: Electric lighting reduced fire hazards and improved visibility, enhancing safety.
- **Leisure and Entertainment**: Electricity powered cinemas, radios, and phonographs, creating new forms of entertainment.

### Economic Expansion

- **Job Creation**: The electrical industry generated employment opportunities, from engineering to manufacturing.
- **Global Trade**: Electrification supported industrial output, boosting international trade and economic integration.

## 5. Challenges and Critiques

While electricity revolutionized society, its development and adoption were not without challenges and controversies.

### Access and Inequality

- **Urban-Rural Divide**: Electrification initially benefited urban areas, leaving rural regions underserved.
- **Economic Disparities**: The high cost of infrastructure limited access for lower-income communities.

### Environmental Concerns

- **Resource Depletion**: Reliance on coal and other fossil fuels for power generation contributed to resource depletion and environmental degradation.
- **Pollution**: Early power plants and industries caused air and water pollution, raising ecological concerns.

**Monopolies and Regulation**

The consolidation of the electrical industry into monopolies raised issues of price control, competition, and government oversight.

## 6. The Global Spread of Electricity

The electrification movement expanded beyond industrialized nations, shaping global development.

**Colonial Impacts**

Colonial powers introduced electrification in their territories, often prioritizing infrastructure that served their economic interests.

**Economic Modernization**

Developing nations embraced electricity as a means of modernizing economies, with electrification projects becoming symbols of progress.

**Cultural Exchange**

The global spread of electrically powered communication, such as telegraphs and telephones, fostered cultural exchange and international cooperation.

## 7. Legacy and Lessons of Electrification

The development of electricity remains one of humanity's most transformative achievements, with enduring implications for the present and future.

**Technological Innovation**

Electricity paved the way for technological advancements in computing, renewable energy, and space exploration.

**Global Connectivity**

Electrification laid the foundation for the digital age, with electronic communication and the internet revolutionizing human interaction.

**Sustainability Challenges**

The environmental impact of electricity generation underscores the need for sustainable energy solutions, such as solar and wind power.

## 8. Conclusion: The Power to Transform

The development of electricity in the 19th century was a pivotal moment in human history, revolutionizing industries, transforming daily life, and shaping the modern world. Its journey from innovation to ubiquity reflects humanity's capacity for ingenuity and adaptation. As we navigate the challenges of the 21st century, the legacy of electrification serves as a reminder of the transformative power of innovation and the need for equitable and sustainable progress.

## The Invention of the Telephone: Connecting the World

### Introduction: The Birth of Modern Communication

The invention of the telephone by Alexander Graham Bell in 1876 marked a pivotal moment in human history. This groundbreaking innovation transformed the way people communicated, breaking barriers of time and distance. By enabling instant connectivity over vast distances, the telephone not only revolutionized personal and business communication but also laid the foundation for the intricate global communication networks we rely on today. This essay delves into the historical context, technological advancements, societal impacts, and enduring legacy of the telephone, charting its evolution and influence on the modern world.

## 1. The Pre-Telephone Era: Communication Across Distance

Before the invention of the telephone, long-distance communication was limited to written correspondence, messengers, and rudimentary electronic systems.

**Traditional Methods**

- **Letters and Couriers**: Written messages were transported by messengers, horses, or ships, often taking days or weeks to reach their destination.
- **Optical Telegraphs**: Systems like semaphore towers used visual signals to transmit messages over short distances, constrained by line-of-sight limitations.

**The Electric Telegraph**

The invention of the electric telegraph in the early 19th century by Samuel Morse and others revolutionized communication by allowing messages to be transmitted over wires using Morse code.

- **Advantages**: The telegraph significantly reduced communication time, enabling near-instantaneous message transmission.
- **Limitations**: Telegraphs required skilled operators and could only transmit textual information.

## 2. The Invention of the Telephone

**Alexander Graham Bell and the Breakthrough**

The telephone was born out of Alexander Graham Bell's experiments with sound and electrical signals. Bell, a teacher of the deaf, was deeply interested in acoustics and the mechanics of speech.

- **Milestone Event**: On March 10, 1876, Bell successfully transmitted the first intelligible sentence: "Mr. Watson, come here, I want to see you."
- **Patent and Controversy**: Bell's patent for the telephone, filed on February 14, 1876, faced challenges from other inventors like Elisha Gray. However, Bell's design ultimately proved superior.

### How the Telephone Worked

Early telephones converted sound waves into electrical signals, transmitted them over wires, and reconverted them into sound waves at the receiving end.

- **Key Components**: The transmitter (microphone), receiver (earpiece), and a conductive wire formed the basic setup.
- **Innovations**: Continuous refinements, such as Thomas Edison's carbon transmitter, improved sound clarity and reliability.

## 3. Early Adoption and Expansion

### Initial Skepticism

The telephone faced skepticism upon its introduction. Many people viewed it as a novelty rather than a practical tool. Businesses and individuals were slow to adopt the technology due to cost and unfamiliarity.

### Building the Network

- **Telephone Exchanges**: The establishment of telephone exchanges in the 1880s enabled multiple users to connect through operators, forming the first communication networks.

- **Long-Distance Lines**: Innovations like metallic circuits and insulating materials allowed the extension of telephone lines over longer distances.

**Bell Telephone Company**

Bell's invention led to the formation of the Bell Telephone Company, which dominated the early telephone industry. The company's aggressive expansion strategy included patent enforcement and infrastructure investment.

## 4. Societal Impacts of the Telephone

**Revolutionizing Communication**

The telephone's ability to provide real-time voice communication transformed how individuals and businesses interacted.

- **Personal Connections**: Families and friends could stay in touch across distances, fostering stronger bonds.
- **Business Efficiency**: Companies could coordinate operations, negotiate deals, and respond to customer inquiries more effectively.

**Economic Growth**

The telephone became a catalyst for economic development, creating new industries and job opportunities.

- **Telecommunication Jobs**: Operators, linemen, and engineers became essential roles.
- **Supporting Industries**: The production of telephone equipment and infrastructure spurred growth in manufacturing and construction.

**Urbanization and Social Change**

The telephone played a role in urbanization by improving communication in densely populated areas.

- **Accessibility**: Urban centers adopted telephone technology more rapidly, enhancing coordination in city planning, emergency response, and public services.
- **Social Integration**: The telephone bridged social and cultural divides, connecting people across class and geographic boundaries.

## 5. The Evolution of Telephone Technology

### From Analog to Digital

The telephone underwent significant technological evolution, transitioning from analog systems to digital networks.

- **Rotary and Touch-Tone Phones**: Early rotary dials gave way to touch-tone phones, simplifying dialing.
- **Digital Switching**: The introduction of digital exchanges improved call quality and network efficiency.

### Wireless Communication

The advent of wireless technology revolutionized telephony, untethering communication from physical wires.

- **Mobile Phones**: Early mobile phones in the 1980s evolved into modern smartphones, integrating internet connectivity and multimedia capabilities.
- **Satellite Communication**: Satellites enabled global connectivity, extending the reach of telephony to remote areas.

### The Internet and VoIP

The rise of the internet introduced Voice over Internet Protocol (VoIP) technology, allowing voice communication over digital networks.

- **Cost Efficiency**: VoIP reduced costs for international and long-distance calls.
- **Integration**: Services like Skype and Zoom merged voice, video, and data communication.

## 6. Global Impact and Connectivity

### Economic Integration

The telephone played a pivotal role in global economic integration, supporting trade, finance, and international collaboration.

- **Multinational Corporations**: Telecommunication networks enabled seamless coordination among global offices.
- **Global Markets**: Real-time communication facilitated faster decision-making and market responses.

### Cultural Exchange

Telephony bridged cultural gaps, enabling people from diverse backgrounds to interact and share ideas.

- **Language Learning**: Telephone communication supported language exchange and cross-cultural understanding.
- **Media and Entertainment**: The telephone laid the groundwork for media distribution and live broadcasts.

### Disaster Response and Relief

Telecommunication infrastructure became critical in disaster response, enabling coordination of relief efforts and emergency services.

# 7. Challenges and Critiques

### Privacy Concerns

The telephone raised issues of privacy and surveillance, as conversations could be monitored or intercepted.

### Monopolies and Regulation

The dominance of companies like Bell led to concerns about monopolistic practices. Governments introduced regulations to ensure fair competition and access.

### Digital Divide

Access to telephony technology varied across regions and socioeconomic groups, highlighting disparities in connectivity.

# 8. The Legacy of the Telephone

### Foundation for Modern Communication

The telephone's principles underpin today's telecommunication systems, from mobile networks to the internet.

- **Technological Convergence**: Modern smartphones combine voice communication with data, video, and applications.
- **Global Connectivity**: The telephone paved the way for a connected world, shaping globalization and cultural exchange.

### Enduring Symbol of Innovation

The telephone remains a symbol of human ingenuity, exemplifying how technology can bridge distances and transform society.

# 9. Conclusion: A World Connected

The invention of the telephone by Alexander Graham Bell was more than a technological breakthrough; it was a transformative force that redefined human interaction and connectivity. From its humble beginnings as a simple voice transmission device to its evolution into the backbone of global communication networks, the telephone has profoundly shaped the modern world. Its legacy endures, reminding us of the power of innovation to unite and empower humanity.

## The Digital Revolution: Redefining the 20th Century and Beyond

### Introduction: A Leap into the Digital Age

The Digital Revolution of the 20th century stands as one of the most transformative periods in human history. Marked by the advent of computers, semiconductors, and digital technology, this era redefined industries, reshaped societies, and fundamentally altered human interaction with information. At its core, the Digital Revolution was not merely a technological shift but a profound societal transformation, touching every facet of life. This essay explores the origins, technological milestones, societal impacts, and enduring legacy of the Digital Revolution, charting its trajectory from the early days of computing to the modern digital age.

# 1. The Foundations of the Digital Revolution

**Early Computing Innovations**

The seeds of the Digital Revolution were sown in the mid-20th century with the development of early computing machines.

- **Mechanical Computers**: Devices like Charles Babbage's Analytical Engine and Alan Turing's conceptual Turing Machine laid the theoretical groundwork for modern computing.
- **World War II Contributions**: Machines like the Colossus and ENIAC, developed for wartime cryptography and calculations, demonstrated the potential of automated computation.

**The Semiconductor Breakthrough**

The invention of the transistor in 1947 by John Bardeen, Walter Brattain, and William Shockley revolutionized electronics.

- **Transition from Vacuum Tubes**: Transistors replaced bulky vacuum tubes, enabling smaller, more efficient electronic devices.
- **Integrated Circuits**: The development of integrated circuits in the 1950s and 1960s by Jack Kilby and Robert Noyce further miniaturized and enhanced electronic components.

**From Analog to Digital**

The shift from analog to digital systems marked a turning point, allowing for precise, efficient, and scalable data processing.

- **Binary Code**: The adoption of binary code, pioneered by George Boole and others, became the foundation of digital communication.

- **Digital Storage**: Magnetic tape, floppy disks, and later hard drives revolutionized data storage and retrieval.

## 2. Key Innovations Driving the Revolution

### The Birth of Personal Computers

The 1970s and 1980s saw the emergence of personal computers, bringing digital technology into homes and small businesses.

- **Pioneering Models**: Early personal computers like the Altair 8800, Apple II, and IBM PC democratized access to computing.
- **Graphical User Interface (GUI)**: Innovations like GUIs, popularized by Apple's Macintosh, made computers more user-friendly.

### The Internet: Connecting the World

The development of the internet transformed communication, commerce, and knowledge dissemination.

- **Origins**: ARPANET, developed in the late 1960s, laid the groundwork for the modern internet.
- **World Wide Web**: Tim Berners-Lee's invention of the World Wide Web in 1989 revolutionized how information was accessed and shared.
- **E-Commerce**: Platforms like Amazon and eBay emerged in the 1990s, reshaping global trade and consumer behavior.

### Mobile and Wireless Technology

The advent of mobile devices and wireless communication extended the reach of digital technology.

- **Mobile Phones**: From early brick-sized models to modern smartphones, mobile devices became essential tools for communication and productivity.
- **Wi-Fi and Cellular Networks**: Wireless technology enabled seamless connectivity, supporting remote work, entertainment, and navigation.

**Automation and Artificial Intelligence**

Advancements in automation and AI redefined industries by streamlining processes and enhancing decision-making.

- **Industrial Robots**: Automated manufacturing systems increased efficiency and precision.
- **Machine Learning**: AI systems capable of analyzing vast datasets found applications in healthcare, finance, and beyond.

## 3. Transforming Industries

The Digital Revolution disrupted and redefined traditional industries, creating new paradigms of operation and value creation.

**Manufacturing**

- **Computer-Aided Design (CAD)**: Digital tools revolutionized product design and prototyping.
- **Smart Factories**: IoT-enabled factories integrated data-driven decision-making into production processes.

**Healthcare**

- **Medical Imaging**: Digital technologies like MRI and CT scans enhanced diagnostic accuracy.
- **Telemedicine**: Digital platforms enabled remote consultations, improving healthcare accessibility.

### Education

- **E-Learning Platforms**: Platforms like Coursera and Khan Academy democratized education, offering courses to a global audience.
- **Digital Classrooms**: Tools like Google Classroom and Zoom transformed traditional learning environments.

### Finance

- **Digital Banking**: Online banking services provided convenience and accessibility.
- **Cryptocurrencies**: Blockchain technology introduced decentralized digital currencies like Bitcoin, challenging traditional financial systems.

## 4. Societal Impacts

### Communication and Social Interaction

Digital technology reshaped how people connect and interact.

- **Social Media**: Platforms like Facebook, Twitter, and Instagram created new avenues for communication and self-expression.
- **Global Communities**: Online forums and groups fostered connections across geographic and cultural boundaries.

### Work and Productivity

The Digital Revolution redefined the workplace, enabling new forms of collaboration and productivity.

- **Remote Work**: Digital tools facilitated remote work, a trend accelerated by the COVID-19 pandemic.
- **Automation**: Routine tasks were automated, freeing human workers for more creative and strategic roles.

## Cultural Shifts

Digital media transformed how art, music, and literature were created, distributed, and consumed.

- **Streaming Services**: Platforms like Netflix and Spotify disrupted traditional entertainment models.
- **User-Generated Content**: Platforms like YouTube and TikTok empowered individuals to become creators.

## 5. Challenges and Critiques

### Digital Divide

Not all communities have equal access to digital technology, exacerbating socioeconomic inequalities.

- **Infrastructure Gaps**: Rural and underdeveloped regions often lack robust digital infrastructure.
- **Skills Disparity**: Digital literacy varies widely, affecting opportunities and inclusion.

### Privacy and Security

The proliferation of digital technology has raised concerns about data privacy and cybersecurity.

- **Surveillance**: Governments and corporations collect vast amounts of user data, sparking debates about privacy rights.
- **Cyber Threats**: Hacking, identity theft, and ransomware attacks pose significant risks.

### Environmental Impact

The energy consumption of data centers and electronic waste generation highlights the environmental challenges of the Digital Revolution.

- **E-Waste**: The rapid obsolescence of devices contributes to growing electronic waste.
- **Energy Usage**: Data centers and blockchain systems require substantial energy resources.

## 6. The Legacy of the Digital Revolution

### Empowering Individuals

The democratization of information and tools has empowered individuals to innovate, create, and share on an unprecedented scale.

### Global Connectivity

Digital technology has woven a web of connectivity, enabling collaboration and understanding across borders.

### Continuous Innovation

The foundations laid by the Digital Revolution continue to drive advancements in AI, quantum computing, and space exploration.

## 7. Looking Ahead: The Future of the Digital Age

The Digital Revolution's trajectory offers insights into future trends and challenges.

- **Sustainability**: Developing energy-efficient technologies and addressing e-waste will be crucial.
- **Ethical AI**: Ensuring AI systems are fair, transparent, and aligned with human values.
- **Global Inclusion**: Bridging the digital divide to create equitable opportunities for all.

### Conclusion: A New Paradigm

The Digital Revolution redefined the 20th century, transforming industries, societies, and cultures. Its innovations laid the groundwork for a future shaped by connectivity, automation, and data-driven decision-making. As humanity navigates the complexities of the digital age, the lessons of this revolution serve as a testament to the transformative power of technology and its potential to drive progress when harnessed responsibly.

# The Internet Revolution: Transforming the World in the 1990s and Beyond

## Introduction: A New Era of Connectivity

The Internet Revolution of the 1990s marks one of the most transformative periods in modern history. Anchored by the development of the World Wide Web and global connectivity, this era reshaped how people access information, interact, and conduct business. The internet democratized information, enabled the rise of e-commerce, and introduced new business models like the gig economy, altering the global socioeconomic landscape. This essay explores the origins, technological breakthroughs, societal impacts, and ongoing legacy of the Internet Revolution, highlighting its profound influence on contemporary life.

## 1. The Foundations of the Internet Revolution

### Early Development of the Internet

The roots of the Internet Revolution trace back to mid-20th century innovations in communication and computing.

- **ARPANET**: Developed in the 1960s by the U.S. Department of Defense, ARPANET was the precursor to the modern internet, enabling data sharing between academic and government institutions.
- **TCP/IP Protocol**: Introduced in the 1980s, the Transmission Control Protocol/Internet Protocol (TCP/IP) standardized data transmission, creating a cohesive global network.

### The Birth of the World Wide Web

In 1989, British scientist Tim Berners-Lee proposed the World Wide Web, a system for organizing and accessing information on the internet.

- **Key Innovations**: The Web introduced hypertext, Uniform Resource Locators (URLs), and the Hypertext Transfer Protocol (HTTP), simplifying navigation and access.
- **Public Launch**: In 1991, the World Wide Web became publicly available, sparking widespread adoption and innovation.

## 2. Key Innovations and Technologies

### Web Browsers

The development of web browsers transformed the internet from a niche tool into a user-friendly platform for the masses.

- **Mosaic (1993)**: The first widely used graphical web browser made the web visually appealing and accessible.
- **Netscape Navigator**: Launched in 1994, Netscape became a dominant browser, driving internet adoption.

**Search Engines**

Search engines revolutionized information retrieval, enabling users to find specific content amid a growing web.

- **Yahoo! and AltaVista**: Early search engines indexed websites, streamlining navigation.
- **Google (1998)**: Google's algorithmic approach to ranking search results redefined the search experience, becoming the dominant platform.

**E-Commerce Platforms**

The 1990s witnessed the rise of e-commerce, redefining retail and business transactions.

- **Amazon (1995)**: Initially an online bookstore, Amazon expanded to become a global retail giant.
- **eBay (1995)**: Pioneering online auctions, eBay facilitated peer-to-peer commerce.

**Social Networking Foundations**

While social media as we know it emerged later, the 1990s laid the groundwork for online communities.

- **Early Platforms**: Sites like GeoCities and forums created spaces for user-generated content and interaction.

## 3. The Impact on Information and Communication

**Democratization of Information**

The internet revolutionized access to information, breaking down barriers to knowledge.

- **Educational Resources**: Online libraries, encyclopedias, and courses made learning accessible to a global audience.
- **Journalism and Media**: Digital news platforms enabled real-time reporting and diversified media consumption.

## Global Communication

The internet transformed how people communicate, fostering instant connectivity across distances.

- **Email**: Replacing traditional mail, email became the primary communication tool for personal and professional use.
- **Instant Messaging**: Platforms like ICQ and AOL Instant Messenger enabled real-time text communication.

## 4. Economic and Business Transformation

### E-Commerce Boom

The internet reshaped retail and consumer behavior, creating new opportunities and challenges.

- **Convenience**: Online shopping offered 24/7 accessibility and personalized recommendations.
- **Global Markets**: Businesses reached international audiences, expanding their customer base.

### Rise of the Gig Economy

The internet enabled new work models, emphasizing flexibility and independence.

- **Freelance Platforms**: Sites like Upwork connected freelancers with clients worldwide.

- **Ride-Sharing and Delivery**: Companies like Uber and DoorDash pioneered app-based gig services.

### Digital Marketing

Businesses adopted digital marketing strategies to target audiences effectively.

- **Search Engine Optimization (SEO)**: Optimizing content for search engines became a critical tool for visibility.
- **Social Media Advertising**: Platforms like Facebook and Instagram revolutionized brand engagement and advertising.

## 5. Societal and Cultural Shifts

### Online Communities and Social Interaction

The internet created virtual spaces for people to connect and share ideas.

- **Forums and Blogs**: Early platforms fostered niche communities and personal expression.
- **Cultural Exchange**: Global connectivity facilitated cross-cultural interaction and understanding.

### Entertainment and Content Creation

The internet transformed entertainment, empowering users as creators and consumers.

- **Streaming Platforms**: Services like Napster and YouTube disrupted traditional media industries.
- **User-Generated Content**: Blogs, videos, and social media posts democratized content creation.

### Political Activism and Social Movements

The internet became a tool for organizing and amplifying social and political causes.

- **Grassroots Campaigns**: Activists used online platforms to mobilize support and share information.
- **Digital Advocacy**: Social media amplified marginalized voices and brought attention to global issues.

## 6. Challenges and Critiques

### Digital Divide

Access to the internet remains unequal, exacerbating existing socioeconomic disparities.

- **Infrastructure Gaps**: Rural and underdeveloped regions often lack reliable connectivity.
- **Affordability**: High costs of devices and services limit access for lower-income populations.

### Privacy and Security Concerns

The internet's growth introduced new risks to personal and organizational security.

- **Data Breaches**: Cyberattacks compromised sensitive information.
- **Surveillance**: Governments and corporations collected user data, raising ethical questions.

### Misinformation and Digital Ethics

The internet's open nature enabled the spread of misinformation and harmful content.

- **Fake News**: False information influenced public opinion and political processes.

- **Online Harassment**: Anonymity facilitated cyberbullying and abusive behavior.

## 7. Legacy and Future Prospects

### Pervasive Connectivity

The Internet Revolution laid the foundation for ubiquitous digital connectivity.

- **Smart Devices**: The Internet of Things (IoT) integrates connectivity into everyday objects.
- **5G Networks**: High-speed wireless networks enhance real-time applications and data transfer.

### Digital Economy

The internet continues to drive innovation and economic growth.

- **Startups and Innovation**: Digital platforms enable entrepreneurs to launch and scale businesses.
- **Global Collaboration**: Virtual tools support international teamwork and knowledge sharing.

### Artificial Intelligence and Automation

The integration of AI and machine learning into internet systems promises new possibilities and challenges.

## Conclusion: A Connected World

The Internet Revolution of the 1990s transformed the global landscape, democratizing access to information and redefining communication, commerce, and culture. Its impact is visible in every aspect of modern life, from how we interact to how we work and learn. As the internet continues to evolve, its legacy reminds us of the immense potential of connectivity and innovation to shape the future.

# The Green Revolution: Transforming Global Agriculture

## Introduction: A Paradigm Shift in Agriculture

The mid-20th century marked a pivotal moment in human history with the advent of the Green Revolution. Spurred by groundbreaking advances in agricultural science, including the development of high-yield crops, synthetic fertilizers, and advanced irrigation techniques, the Green Revolution addressed food shortages that had plagued many parts of the world for centuries. This transformative era not only alleviated hunger but also enabled rapid population growth and enhanced global stability. However, the Green Revolution also brought with it a complex legacy of environmental, social, and economic challenges. This essay explores the origins, innovations, impacts, and long-term consequences of the Green Revolution, charting its profound influence on global agriculture and society.

## 1. The Context: A World on the Brink of Hunger

### Population Growth and Food Insecurity

By the early 20th century, population growth outpaced agricultural production in many regions, leading to widespread food shortages and famine.

- **The Malthusian Dilemma**: Economist Thomas Malthus theorized that population growth would outstrip food supply, causing periodic famine.

- **Post-War Challenges**: World War II exacerbated global food insecurity, with disrupted supply chains and devastated farmland.

## Traditional Farming Limitations

Conventional farming methods were labor-intensive and relied heavily on natural weather patterns and soil fertility.

- **Low Crop Yields**: Traditional crops produced limited yields, making it difficult to meet rising demand.
- **Vulnerability to Pests and Diseases**: Crops were often decimated by pests, diseases, and adverse weather conditions.

## 2. The Innovations of the Green Revolution

### High-Yield Crop Varieties

The development of high-yielding varieties (HYVs) of staple crops like wheat, rice, and maize was a cornerstone of the Green Revolution.

- **Norman Borlaug's Contribution**: Known as the "Father of the Green Revolution," Borlaug developed disease-resistant, high-yield wheat varieties.
- **Global Adoption**: Countries like Mexico, India, and the Philippines saw dramatic increases in agricultural output after adopting HYVs.

### Synthetic Fertilizers and Pesticides

Chemical advancements provided farmers with tools to enhance soil fertility and protect crops from pests.

- **Nitrogen-Based Fertilizers**: These fertilizers supplied essential nutrients to crops, boosting growth and yield.

- **Chemical Pesticides**: Pesticides reduced crop losses due to pests and diseases, ensuring higher productivity.

## Mechanization and Irrigation

Technological advancements in farming equipment and water management revolutionized traditional agriculture.

- **Tractors and Harvesters**: Mechanized equipment reduced labor requirements and increased efficiency.
- **Irrigation Systems**: Innovations like drip irrigation and tube wells ensured consistent water supply, mitigating the effects of drought.

# 3. Global Impacts of the Green Revolution

## Increased Agricultural Productivity

The Green Revolution significantly boosted food production, particularly in developing countries.

- **Wheat and Rice Surpluses**: Countries like India and Pakistan transitioned from food scarcity to self-sufficiency.
- **Export Opportunities**: Surpluses enabled some nations to become exporters of staple crops.

## Population Growth and Urbanization

Improved food security contributed to rapid population growth and urban development.

- **Reduced Famine**: The prevalence of large-scale famines declined in many parts of the world.
- **Urban Migration**: Surplus labor from rural areas migrated to cities, fueling industrialization.

## Economic Development

Agricultural surpluses spurred economic growth and diversification.

- **Rural Prosperity**: Increased incomes for farmers and agricultural workers improved living standards.
- **Industrial Growth**: Enhanced agricultural productivity supported industrial development through surplus labor and raw materials.

## 4. Environmental Consequences

While the Green Revolution addressed immediate food shortages, it also introduced significant environmental challenges.

**Soil Degradation**

Intensive farming practices depleted soil nutrients, reducing long-term fertility.

- **Overuse of Fertilizers**: Excessive application of synthetic fertilizers led to soil acidification and nutrient imbalances.
- **Erosion**: Monoculture farming increased soil erosion, undermining agricultural sustainability.

**Water Scarcity**

Irrigation-intensive farming strained water resources, particularly in arid regions.

- **Depleted Aquifers**: Over-reliance on groundwater led to falling water tables in key agricultural areas.
- **Pollution**: Runoff from fertilizers and pesticides contaminated water bodies, affecting ecosystems and human health.

**Loss of Biodiversity**

The focus on high-yield crops reduced agricultural biodiversity.

- **Genetic Erosion**: Traditional crop varieties were abandoned in favor of HYVs, narrowing genetic diversity.
- **Habitat Destruction**: Expansion of farmland encroached on natural habitats, threatening wildlife.

## 5. Social and Economic Critiques

### Uneven Benefits

The Green Revolution's benefits were not evenly distributed, exacerbating existing inequalities.

- **Wealth Disparities**: Wealthier farmers with access to resources benefited more than smallholders.
- **Land Concentration**: Mechanization and capital-intensive farming led to the consolidation of landholdings.

### Marginalization of Small Farmers

Small-scale farmers often lacked access to the technologies and inputs necessary to compete.

- **Debt Traps**: Many smallholders incurred debts to purchase seeds, fertilizers, and equipment.
- **Displacement**: Mechanization reduced labor demand, displacing rural workers.

### Cultural Impacts

Traditional farming practices and indigenous knowledge systems were sidelined.

- **Erosion of Traditions**: The focus on modern techniques undermined traditional agricultural practices.
- **Dependency**: Farmers became reliant on external inputs like hybrid seeds and chemical fertilizers.

## 6. The Legacy of the Green Revolution

**Global Food Security**

The Green Revolution's contributions to food security remain a cornerstone of its legacy.

- **Hunger Alleviation**: Millions were lifted out of hunger, particularly in Asia and Latin America.
- **Stabilized Markets**: Increased production reduced food price volatility, benefiting consumers globally.

**Agricultural Research and Development**

The Green Revolution spurred ongoing innovation in agricultural science.

- **Biotechnology**: Advances in genetic engineering have built on the Green Revolution's foundation.
- **Sustainable Practices**: Efforts to address environmental and social critiques have led to more sustainable farming approaches.

## 7. Looking Ahead: Toward a Sustainable Green Revolution

**Integrating Technology and Sustainability**

Future agricultural innovations must balance productivity with environmental stewardship.

- **Precision Agriculture**: Technologies like GPS and drones optimize resource use and reduce waste.
- **Agroecology**: Integrating ecological principles into farming can enhance resilience and biodiversity.

**Empowering Small Farmers**

Inclusive policies and programs can ensure that smallholders benefit from modern agricultural advances.

- **Access to Credit**: Financial support can help small farmers invest in sustainable practices.
- **Knowledge Sharing**: Training and extension services can bridge the gap between traditional and modern techniques.

**Addressing Climate Change**

Agriculture must adapt to the challenges posed by a changing climate.

- **Climate-Resilient Crops**: Developing drought- and heat-tolerant varieties is critical.
- **Carbon Sequestration**: Promoting practices like agroforestry can mitigate agriculture's carbon footprint.

## Conclusion: A Revolution with a Complex Legacy

The Green Revolution represents a remarkable achievement in human ingenuity and problem-solving, addressing critical food shortages and enabling global population growth and stability. However, its environmental and social consequences underscore the need for a more holistic approach to agricultural development. As we look to the future, the lessons of the Green Revolution can guide us toward a sustainable and inclusive path, ensuring food security for generations to come.

68

# Artificial Intelligence and Machine Learning: Transforming the 21st Century

## Introduction: The Rise of Intelligent Machines

The 21st century has been defined by the rapid development and adoption of Artificial Intelligence (AI) and Machine Learning (ML). These technologies, driven by advanced algorithms and exponential growth in computational power, have transformed industries, reshaped economies, and altered daily life. AI and ML are not just tools; they represent a paradigm shift in how humans interact with technology, process information, and solve problems. From enabling automation to delivering predictive analytics and personalized services, these innovations have far-reaching implications. This essay delves into the history, technological breakthroughs, industrial applications, societal impacts, and future potential of AI and ML.

## 1. The Foundations of Artificial Intelligence and Machine Learning

### The Origins of AI

AI as a concept has existed for decades, with its formalization beginning in the mid-20th century.

- **The Dartmouth Conference (1956)**: Considered the birth of AI as a field, researchers proposed that machines could simulate human intelligence.
- **Early Milestones**: Programs like ELIZA (a simple natural language processor) and the development of rule-based systems laid the groundwork for AI.

## The Evolution of Machine Learning

Machine Learning, a subset of AI, focuses on enabling machines to learn from data and improve their performance without explicit programming.

- **Statistical Foundations**: ML emerged from statistical methods, such as regression analysis and decision trees.
- **Neural Networks**: Inspired by the human brain, neural networks became a cornerstone of ML, enabling pattern recognition and data classification.

## Technological Enablers

Several technological advancements have propelled AI and ML into the mainstream:

- **Moore's Law**: Exponential growth in computational power made complex algorithms feasible.
- **Big Data**: The proliferation of digital data provided the fuel for training ML models.
- **Cloud Computing**: Scalable and affordable cloud infrastructure enabled widespread experimentation and deployment of AI systems.

# 2. Key Innovations and Breakthroughs

## Deep Learning

Deep learning, a subset of ML, involves neural networks with multiple layers, allowing systems to process unstructured data like images and speech.

- **Convolutional Neural Networks (CNNs)**: Revolutionized image recognition and computer vision.
- **Recurrent Neural Networks (RNNs)**: Advanced natural language processing and time-series analysis.

## Natural Language Processing (NLP)

NLP enables machines to understand, interpret, and respond to human language.

- **Transformers**: Models like GPT and BERT revolutionized NLP, powering chatbots, translation tools, and content generation.
- **Sentiment Analysis**: Widely used in social media monitoring and customer feedback systems.

## Reinforcement Learning

Reinforcement learning focuses on training agents to make decisions by interacting with their environment.

- **AlphaGo**: Demonstrated the power of reinforcement learning by defeating world champions in the game of Go.
- **Autonomous Systems**: Applied in robotics and self-driving cars.

# 3. Industry Applications

## Healthcare

AI and ML are revolutionizing healthcare, improving diagnostics, treatment planning, and patient outcomes.

- **Medical Imaging**: AI models detect diseases like cancer with high accuracy in X-rays and MRIs.
- **Personalized Medicine**: Predictive analytics tailor treatments to individual genetic profiles.
- **Operational Efficiency**: Automated scheduling and resource allocation streamline hospital operations.

## Finance

The finance industry has embraced AI for risk assessment, fraud detection, and customer engagement.

- **Algorithmic Trading**: ML algorithms analyze market data in real-time to execute trades.
- **Credit Scoring**: AI evaluates creditworthiness more accurately than traditional models.
- **Fraud Prevention**: Systems identify suspicious transactions using pattern recognition.

**Retail and E-Commerce**

AI has transformed retail by enhancing customer experiences and optimizing operations.

- **Recommendation Engines**: Personalized product suggestions increase customer engagement.
- **Inventory Management**: Predictive analytics optimize stock levels, reducing waste.
- **Chatbots**: AI-driven customer service agents provide instant support.

**Manufacturing**

Automation powered by AI has streamlined production processes and quality control.

- **Predictive Maintenance**: Sensors and ML models predict equipment failures, minimizing downtime.
- **Robotics**: Intelligent robots perform complex tasks with precision.
- **Supply Chain Optimization**: AI enhances logistics and demand forecasting.

**Transportation**

AI and ML are driving innovations in mobility and logistics.

- **Autonomous Vehicles**: Self-driving cars and drones use AI for navigation and obstacle avoidance.
- **Traffic Management**: AI optimizes traffic flow and reduces congestion.
- **Delivery Optimization**: Logistics companies use AI to plan efficient delivery routes.

## 4. Societal Impacts

### Economic Transformation

AI and ML have reshaped economies, creating new industries while disrupting traditional ones.

- **Job Creation and Displacement**: While automation has eliminated some jobs, it has also created demand for AI-related roles.
- **Productivity Gains**: Automation and data-driven decision-making have increased efficiency across sectors.

### Ethical and Privacy Concerns

The widespread use of AI raises significant ethical and privacy issues.

- **Bias in Algorithms**: ML models can perpetuate societal biases present in training data.
- **Data Privacy**: The collection and use of personal data by AI systems raise concerns about consent and security.
- **Accountability**: Determining responsibility for AI-driven decisions remains a challenge.

### Global Inequalities

Access to AI technology varies widely, exacerbating existing inequalities.

- **Digital Divide**: Developing nations often lack the infrastructure to leverage AI.
- **Resource Inequity**: Wealthier organizations dominate AI development, concentrating power.

### Cultural and Social Changes

AI has influenced culture and social dynamics, from entertainment to human relationships.

- **Content Creation**: AI generates art, music, and writing, sparking debates about creativity.
- **Human Interaction**: AI-powered virtual assistants and social media algorithms shape how people connect.

## 5. Challenges and Critiques

### Technical Limitations

Despite advancements, AI and ML face challenges in achieving general intelligence and reliability.

- **Explainability**: Complex models like deep learning are often seen as "black boxes," making their decisions difficult to interpret.
- **Data Dependency**: High-quality, labeled data is essential for training AI systems, limiting their application in data-scarce environments.

### Regulation and Governance

Governments and organizations struggle to keep pace with the rapid development of AI.

- **Ethical Standards**: Establishing guidelines for fair and responsible AI use is an ongoing challenge.

- **Regulatory Frameworks**: Policies must balance innovation with safeguards against misuse.

### Environmental Impact

Training large AI models requires significant computational resources, contributing to energy consumption.

- **Carbon Footprint**: Data centers and training processes generate substantial greenhouse gas emissions.
- **Sustainability Initiatives**: Efforts are underway to develop energy-efficient AI systems.

## 6. The Future of AI and Machine Learning

### Advancements in General AI

Researchers aim to create systems with general intelligence, capable of understanding and performing diverse tasks at human levels.

- **Multi-Modal Learning**: Integrating text, image, and audio processing for versatile applications.
- **Ethical AI**: Building systems that align with human values and societal goals.

### AI in Climate Change Mitigation

AI can play a critical role in addressing environmental challenges.

- **Renewable Energy Optimization**: AI improves the efficiency of solar and wind power systems.
- **Environmental Monitoring**: Satellite data and AI models track deforestation, pollution, and climate patterns.

### Human-AI Collaboration

The future will likely emphasize collaborative systems where AI augments human capabilities.

- **Augmented Intelligence**: AI tools assist professionals in medicine, education, and engineering.
- **Democratization of AI**: Accessible platforms enable non-experts to harness AI for innovation.

## Conclusion: A Transformative Force

Artificial Intelligence and Machine Learning have redefined the 21st century, revolutionizing industries, enhancing decision-making, and reshaping society. While challenges remain, from ethical dilemmas to technical limitations, the potential of AI and ML to drive progress and innovation is unparalleled. As humanity continues to explore and harness these technologies, balancing their benefits with responsible use will be essential to ensuring a future where AI serves as a force for good.

## Quantum Computing: Unlocking the Power of Quantum Mechanics

## Introduction: The Quantum Leap in Computing

Quantum computing, an emerging field at the intersection of physics and computer science, represents a revolutionary approach to processing information. By harnessing the principles of quantum mechanics, quantum computers hold the promise of solving problems deemed intractable for classical computers. From breakthroughs in cryptography to advances in material science and pharmaceuticals, quantum computing is poised to transform multiple industries at an unprecedented scale. This essay explores the scientific foundations, technological advancements, potential applications, and challenges of quantum computing, as well as its far-reaching implications for the future.

# 1. The Foundations of Quantum Computing

### Quantum Mechanics: A New Paradigm

Quantum computing is rooted in the principles of quantum mechanics, which describe the behavior of particles at atomic and subatomic scales.

- **Superposition**: Unlike classical bits, which are binary (0 or 1), quantum bits, or qubits, can exist in multiple states simultaneously.
- **Entanglement**: Qubits can become entangled, meaning the state of one qubit is directly related to the state of another, even across large distances.
- **Quantum Interference**: Quantum algorithms leverage interference patterns to amplify correct solutions and cancel out incorrect ones.

### The Birth of Quantum Computing

The conceptualization of quantum computing began in the 1980s.

- **Richard Feynman (1981)**: Proposed that quantum systems could be simulated using quantum computers.
- **David Deutsch (1985)**: Demonstrated the theoretical potential of quantum computers with the development of a universal quantum computing model.

# 2. Key Innovations and Advancements

### Quantum Hardware

Building functional quantum computers has required groundbreaking innovations in hardware design.

- **Superconducting Qubits**: Used by companies like IBM and Google, these qubits are maintained at near-absolute-zero temperatures to minimize noise.
- **Trapped Ions**: IonQ and others use ions trapped in electromagnetic fields as qubits, offering stability and precision.
- **Photonic Quantum Computing**: Leveraging photons, this approach eliminates the need for extreme cooling.

## Quantum Algorithms

Quantum algorithms provide the instructions for solving problems using quantum computers.

- **Shor's Algorithm (1994)**: Demonstrated exponential speedup in factoring large numbers, posing a challenge to classical cryptography.
- **Grover's Algorithm**: Offers quadratic speedup for unstructured search problems.
- **Variational Quantum Eigensolver (VQE)**: Used for simulating molecular structures and chemical reactions.

## Quantum Error Correction

Error correction is critical due to the fragile nature of qubits.

- **Surface Codes**: Techniques for detecting and correcting errors in quantum systems.
- **Fault-Tolerant Architectures**: Designs that ensure reliable computation despite noisy qubits.

# 3. Transformative Applications of Quantum Computing

## Cryptography

Quantum computing poses both challenges and opportunities for cryptography.

- **Breaking Classical Encryption**: Shor's algorithm can break widely used encryption methods like RSA.
- **Quantum-Safe Cryptography**: Developing new cryptographic protocols resistant to quantum attacks is a growing field.

## Material Science and Chemistry

Quantum computing can simulate complex molecular systems with unparalleled accuracy.

- **Drug Discovery**: Accelerates the identification of promising compounds and reduces the cost of pharmaceutical development.
- **New Materials**: Enables the design of advanced materials for applications in energy storage, electronics, and more.

## Optimization Problems

Quantum computers excel at solving complex optimization problems in various industries.

- **Supply Chain Management**: Optimizes routes and inventory levels.
- **Finance**: Enhances portfolio optimization and risk analysis.

## Artificial Intelligence and Machine Learning

Quantum computing augments traditional AI and ML techniques.

- **Quantum Neural Networks**: Improves training efficiency for large-scale models.

- **Pattern Recognition**: Enhances image and speech recognition capabilities.

## 4. Challenges in Quantum Computing

### Technical Hurdles

The development of quantum computers faces significant technical challenges.

- **Qubit Stability**: Qubits are highly sensitive to environmental disturbances, leading to decoherence.
- **Scalability**: Building quantum systems with thousands or millions of qubits remains a significant engineering challenge.

### Access and Cost

Quantum computing infrastructure is expensive and accessible primarily to large corporations and research institutions.

- **High Costs**: Maintaining quantum systems requires specialized facilities and expertise.
- **Cloud-Based Solutions**: Companies like IBM and Amazon offer cloud access to quantum systems, democratizing availability.

### Workforce Development

The nascent field requires a highly skilled workforce trained in quantum physics, computer science, and engineering.

- **Educational Programs**: Universities and companies are developing courses and certifications to address the talent gap.
- **Interdisciplinary Collaboration**: Teams must integrate expertise from multiple domains to advance the field.

## 5. Societal and Ethical Implications

### Economic Disruption

Quantum computing could disrupt industries by enabling new technologies and rendering existing systems obsolete.

- **Competitive Advantage**: Early adopters may gain significant economic and geopolitical power.
- **Job Displacement**: Automation of complex tasks could displace certain roles while creating new opportunities.

### Security Concerns

The ability of quantum computers to break encryption poses national and global security risks.

- **Data Vulnerability**: Sensitive information secured by current encryption methods could be exposed.
- **Post-Quantum Security**: Governments and organizations are racing to develop quantum-resistant encryption.

### Ethical Considerations

The immense power of quantum computing raises ethical questions about its use and potential misuse.

- **Equitable Access**: Ensuring that the benefits of quantum computing are shared globally.
- **Misuse Prevention**: Developing frameworks to prevent malicious applications.

## 6. The Future of Quantum Computing

### Short-Term Developments

In the near term, quantum computing will complement classical computing for specific applications.

- **Hybrid Systems**: Combining quantum and classical systems to tackle complex problems.
- **Benchmarking Progress**: Establishing performance benchmarks to measure quantum advantage.

**Long-Term Potential**

In the long term, fully realized quantum computers could revolutionize science, technology, and society.

- **Universal Quantum Computing**: Achieving fault-tolerant, scalable systems capable of tackling any computational problem.
- **Global Collaboration**: International partnerships to accelerate research and address global challenges.

## Conclusion: A Quantum Leap Forward

Quantum computing represents a paradigm shift in technology, unlocking capabilities that were once considered impossible. While still in its infancy, the field has demonstrated transformative potential across industries such as cryptography, material science, and artificial intelligence. However, realizing this potential requires overcoming significant technical, economic, and ethical challenges. As research and development progress, quantum computing has the power to reshape the future, offering solutions to some of humanity's most pressing problems and opening new frontiers of knowledge and innovation.

www.ingramcontent.com/pod-product-compliance
Lightning Source LLC
Chambersburg PA
CBHW062117220526
45471CB00010B/3765